Iman Essence

_To:_

Mommy

From:

3/ 3/ 2021

Date:

Christian art gifts®

Create in me a pure heart, O God, and renew
a steadfast spirit within me. Ps. 51:10

If anyone is in Christ, he is a new creation;
the old has gone, the new has come! 2 Cor. 5:17

Cast your cares on the LORD and He will sustain you.

Ps. 55:22

The LORD your God is with you, He is mighty
to save. He will take great delight in you,
He will quiet you with His love. Zeph. 3:17

The LORD is faithful to all His promises
and loving toward all He has made. Ps. 145:13

In You, O LORD, do I put my trust. Ps. 71:1

"Be strong and courageous. . . . The LORD your God
will be with you wherever you go." Josh. 1:9

Depend on the LORD in whatever you do,
and your plans will succeed. Prov. 16:3

Since we have been justified through faith, we have peace
with God through our LORD Jesus Christ.

Rom. 5:1

The LORD is my rock, my fortress and my deliverer;
my God is my rock, in whom I take refuge. Ps. 18:2

"If anyone would come after Me, he must deny himself
and take up his cross and follow Me." Matt. 16:24

The word of the LORD is right and true;
He is faithful in all He does. Ps. 33:4

The LORD is my strength, my shield from every
danger. I trust in Him with all my heart. Ps. 28:7

In Him we have redemption through His blood,
the forgiveness of sins, in accordance with
the riches of God's grace. Eph. 1:7

I trust in Your unfailing love. I will rejoice
because You have rescued me. Ps. 13:5

Live a life of love, just as Christ loved us and
gave Himself up for us. Eph. 5:2

"You will call upon Me and come and pray to Me, and I will listen to you.
You will seek Me and find Me when you seek Me with all your heart."

Jer. 29:12-13

My soul finds rest in God alone;
My salvation comes from Him. Ps. 62:1

Delight yourself in the LORD, and He will give
you the desires of your heart. Ps. 37:4

The LORD is my light and my salvation–whom shall I fear?
The LORD is the stronghold of my life–of whom shall I be afraid?

Ps. 27:1

The LORD Himself goes before you and will be with you; He will never leave you nor forsake you.

Deut. 31:8

God is working in you, giving you the desire to
obey Him and the power to do what pleases Him.

Phil. 2:13

I can do everything through Christ,
who gives me strength.

Phil. 4:13

If you want to know what God wants you to do,
ask Him, and He will gladly tell you. James 1:5

Create in me a pure heart, O God, and renew
a steadfast spirit within me. Ps. 51:10

If anyone is in Christ, he is a new creation;
the old has gone, the new has come! 2 Cor. 5:17

Cast your cares on the LORD and He will sustain you.

Ps. 55:22

The LORD your God is with you, He is mighty
to save. He will take great delight in you,
He will quiet you with His love. Zeph. 3:17

The LORD is faithful to all His promises
and loving toward all He has made. Ps. 145:13

In You, O LORD, do I put my trust. Ps. 71:1

"Be strong and courageous. . . . The LORD your God
will be with you wherever you go." Josh. 1:9

Depend on the LORD in whatever you do,
and your plans will succeed. Prov. 16:3

Since we have been justified through faith, we have peace
with God through our LORD Jesus Christ.

Rom. 5:1

The LORD is my rock, my fortress and my deliverer;
my God is my rock, in whom I take refuge. Ps. 18:2

"If anyone would come after Me, he must deny himself
and take up his cross and follow Me." Matt. 16:24

The word of the LORD is right and true;
He is faithful in all He does. Ps. 33:4

The LORD is my strength, my shield from every danger. I trust in Him with all my heart. Ps. 28:7

In Him we have redemption through His blood,
the forgiveness of sins, in accordance with
the riches of God's grace. Eph. 1:7

I trust in Your unfailing love. I will rejoice
because You have rescued me. Ps. 13:5

Live a life of love, just as Christ loved us and
gave Himself up for us. Eph. 5:2

"You will call upon Me and come and pray to Me, and I will listen to you.
You will seek Me and find Me when you seek Me with all your heart."

Jer. 29:12-13

My soul finds rest in God alone;
My salvation comes from Him. Ps. 62:1

Delight yourself in the LORD, and He will give
you the desires of your heart. Ps. 37:4

The LORD is my light and my salvation–whom shall I fear?
The LORD is the stronghold of my life–of whom shall I be afraid?

Ps. 27:1

The LORD Himself goes before you and will be with you; He will never leave you nor forsake you.

Deut. 31:8

God is working in you, giving you the desire to
obey Him and the power to do what pleases Him.

Phil. 2:13

I can do everything through Christ,
who gives me strength.

Phil. 4:13

If you want to know what God wants you to do,
ask Him, and He will gladly tell you. James 1:5

Create in me a pure heart, O God, and renew
a steadfast spirit within me. Ps. 51:10

If anyone is in Christ, he is a new creation;
the old has gone, the new has come! 2 Cor. 5:17

Cast your cares on the LORD and He will sustain you.

Ps. 55:22

The LORD your God is with you, He is mighty
to save. He will take great delight in you,
He will quiet you with His love. Zeph. 3:17

The LORD is faithful to all His promises
and loving toward all He has made. Ps. 145:13

In You, O LORD, do I put my trust. Ps. 71:1

"Be strong and courageous. . . . The LORD your God
will be with you wherever you go." Josh. 1:9

Depend on the LORD in whatever you do,
and your plans will succeed. Prov. 16:3

Since we have been justified through faith, we have peace
with God through our LORD Jesus Christ.

Rom. 5:1

The LORD is my rock, my fortress and my deliverer;
my God is my rock, in whom I take refuge. Ps. 18:2

"If anyone would come after Me, he must deny himself
and take up his cross and follow Me." Matt. 16:24

The word of the LORD is right and true;
He is faithful in all He does. Ps. 33:4

The LORD is my strength, my shield from every danger. I trust in Him with all my heart. Ps. 28:7

In Him we have redemption through His blood,
the forgiveness of sins, in accordance with
the riches of God's grace. Eph. 1:7

I trust in Your unfailing love. I will rejoice
because You have rescued me. Ps. 13:5

Live a life of love, just as Christ loved us and
gave Himself up for us. Eph. 5:2

"You will call upon Me and come and pray to Me, and I will listen to you.
You will seek Me and find Me when you seek Me with all your heart."

Jer. 29:12-13

My soul finds rest in God alone;
My salvation comes from Him. Ps. 62:1

Delight yourself in the LORD, and He will give
you the desires of your heart. Ps. 37:4

The LORD is my light and my salvation–whom shall I fear?

The LORD is the stronghold of my life–of whom shall I be afraid?

Ps. 27:1

The LORD Himself goes before you and will be with you; He will never leave you nor forsake you.

Deut. 31:8

God is working in you, giving you the desire to
obey Him and the power to do what pleases Him.

Phil. 2:13

I can do everything through Christ,
who gives me strength.

Phil. 4:13

If you want to know what God wants you to do,
ask Him, and He will gladly tell you. James 1:5

Create in me a pure heart, O God, and renew
a steadfast spirit within me. Ps. 51:10

If anyone is in Christ, he is a new creation;
the old has gone, the new has come! 2 Cor. 5:17

Cast your cares on the LORD and He will sustain you.

Ps. 55:22

The LORD your God is with you, He is mighty
to save. He will take great delight in you,
He will quiet you with His love. Zeph. 3:17

The LORD is faithful to all His promises
and loving toward all He has made. Ps. 145:13

In You, O LORD, do I put my trust. Ps. 71:1

"Be strong and courageous. . . . The LORD your God
will be with you wherever you go." Josh. 1:9

Depend on the LORD in whatever you do,
and your plans will succeed. Prov. 16:3

Since we have been justified through faith, we have peace
with God through our LORD Jesus Christ.

Rom. 5:1

The LORD is my rock, my fortress and my deliverer;
my God is my rock, in whom I take refuge. Ps. 18:2

"If anyone would come after Me, he must deny himself
and take up his cross and follow Me." Matt. 16:24

The word of the LORD is right and true;

He is faithful in all He does. Ps. 33:4

The LORD is my strength, my shield from every
danger. I trust in Him with all my heart. Ps. 28:7

In Him we have redemption through His blood,
the forgiveness of sins, in accordance with
the riches of God's grace. Eph. 1:7

I trust in Your unfailing love. I will rejoice
because You have rescued me. Ps. 13:5

Live a life of love, just as Christ loved us and
gave Himself up for us. Eph. 5:2

"You will call upon Me and come and pray to Me, and I will listen to you. You will seek Me and find Me when you seek Me with all your heart."

Jer. 29:12-13

My soul finds rest in God alone;
My salvation comes from Him. Ps. 62:1

Delight yourself in the LORD, and He will give
you the desires of your heart. Ps. 37:4

The LORD is my light and my salvation–whom shall I fear?

The LORD is the stronghold of my life–of whom shall I be afraid?

Ps. 27:1

The LORD Himself goes before you and will be with you; He will never leave you nor forsake you.

Deut. 31:8

God is working in you, giving you the desire to
obey Him and the power to do what pleases Him.

Phil. 2:13

I can do everything through Christ,
who gives me strength.

Phil. 4:13

If you want to know what God wants you to do,
ask Him, and He will gladly tell you. James 1:5

Create in me a pure heart, O God, and renew
a steadfast spirit within me. Ps. 51:10

If anyone is in Christ, he is a new creation;
the old has gone, the new has come! 2 Cor. 5:17

Cast your cares on the LORD and He will sustain you.

Ps. 55:22

The LORD your God is with you, He is mighty
to save. He will take great delight in you,
He will quiet you with His love. Zeph. 3:17

The LORD is faithful to all His promises
and loving toward all He has made. Ps. 145:13

In You, O LORD, do I put my trust. Ps. 71:1

"Be strong and courageous. . . . The LORD your God
will be with you wherever you go." Josh. 1:9

Depend on the LORD in whatever you do,
and your plans will succeed. Prov. 16:3

Since we have been justified through faith, we have peace
with God through our LORD Jesus Christ.

Rom. 5:1

The LORD is my rock, my fortress and my deliverer;
my God is my rock, in whom I take refuge. Ps. 18:2

"If anyone would come after Me, he must deny himself
and take up his cross and follow Me." Matt. 16:24

The word of the LORD is right and true;
He is faithful in all He does. Ps. 33:4

The LORD is my strength, my shield from every
danger. I trust in Him with all my heart. Ps. 28:7

In Him we have redemption through His blood,
the forgiveness of sins, in accordance with
the riches of God's grace. Eph. 1:7

I trust in Your unfailing love. I will rejoice
because You have rescued me. Ps. 13:5

Live a life of love, just as Christ loved us and
gave Himself up for us. Eph. 5:2

"You will call upon Me and come and pray to Me, and I will listen to you.
You will seek Me and find Me when you seek Me with all your heart."

Jer. 29:12-13

My soul finds rest in God alone;
My salvation comes from Him. Ps. 62:1

Delight yourself in the LORD, and He will give
you the desires of your heart. Ps. 37:4

The LORD is my light and my salvation—whom shall I fear?
The LORD is the stronghold of my life—of whom shall I be afraid?

Ps. 27:1

The LORD Himself goes before you and will be with you; He will never leave you nor forsake you.

Deut. 31:8

God is working in you, giving you the desire to
obey Him and the power to do what pleases Him.

Phil. 2:13

I can do everything through Christ,
who gives me strength.

Phil. 4:13

If you want to know what God wants you to do,
ask Him, and He will gladly tell you. James 1:5

Create in me a pure heart, O God, and renew
a steadfast spirit within me. Ps. 51:10

If anyone is in Christ, he is a new creation;
the old has gone, the new has come! 2 Cor. 5:17

Cast your cares on the LORD and He will sustain you.

Ps. 55:22

The LORD your God is with you, He is mighty
to save. He will take great delight in you,
He will quiet you with His love. Zeph. 3:17

The LORD is faithful to all His promises
and loving toward all He has made. Ps. 145:13

In You, O LORD, do I put my trust. Ps. 71:1

"Be strong and courageous. . . . The LORD your God
will be with you wherever you go." Josh. 1:9

Depend on the LORD in whatever you do,
and your plans will succeed. Prov. 16:3

Since we have been justified through faith, we have peace
with God through our LORD Jesus Christ.

Rom. 5:1

The LORD is my rock, my fortress and my deliverer;
my God is my rock, in whom I take refuge. Ps. 18:2

"If anyone would come after Me, he must deny himself
and take up his cross and follow Me." Matt. 16:24

The word of the LORD is right and true;
He is faithful in all He does. Ps. 33:4

The LORD is my strength, my shield from every
danger. I trust in Him with all my heart. Ps. 28:7

In Him we have redemption through His blood,
the forgiveness of sins, in accordance with
the riches of God's grace. Eph. 1:7

I trust in Your unfailing love. I will rejoice
because You have rescued me. Ps. 13:5

Live a life of love, just as Christ loved us and
gave Himself up for us. Eph. 5:2

"You will call upon Me and come and pray to Me, and I will listen to you.
You will seek Me and find Me when you seek Me with all your heart."

Jer. 29:12-13

My soul finds rest in God alone;
My salvation comes from Him. Ps. 62:1

Delight yourself in the LORD, and He will give
you the desires of your heart. Ps. 37:4

The LORD is my light and my salvation—whom shall I fear?

The LORD is the stronghold of my life—of whom shall I be afraid?

Ps. 27:1

The LORD Himself goes before you and will be with you; He will never leave you nor forsake you.

Deut. 31:8

God is working in you, giving you the desire to
obey Him and the power to do what pleases Him.

Phil. 2:13

I can do everything through Christ,
who gives me strength.

Phil. 4:13

If you want to know what God wants you to do,
ask Him, and He will gladly tell you. James 1:5

Create in me a pure heart, O God, and renew
a steadfast spirit within me. Ps. 51:10

If anyone is in Christ, he is a new creation;
the old has gone, the new has come! 2 Cor. 5:17

Cast your cares on the LORD and He will sustain you.

Ps. 55:22

The LORD your God is with you, He is mighty
to save. He will take great delight in you,
He will quiet you with His love. Zeph. 3:17

The LORD is faithful to all His promises
and loving toward all He has made. Ps. 145:13

In You, O LORD, do I put my trust. Ps. 71:1

"Be strong and courageous. . . . The LORD your God
will be with you wherever you go." Josh. 1:9

Depend on the LORD in whatever you do,
and your plans will succeed. Prov. 16:3

Since we have been justified through faith, we have peace
with God through our LORD Jesus Christ.

Rom. 5:1

The LORD is my rock, my fortress and my deliverer;
my God is my rock, in whom I take refuge. Ps. 18:2

"If anyone would come after Me, he must deny himself
and take up his cross and follow Me." Matt. 16:24

The word of the LORD is right and true;
He is faithful in all He does. Ps. 33:4

The LORD is my strength, my shield from every
danger. I trust in Him with all my heart. Ps. 28:7

In Him we have redemption through His blood,
the forgiveness of sins, in accordance with
the riches of God's grace. Eph. 1:7

I trust in Your unfailing love. I will rejoice
because You have rescued me. Ps. 13:5

Live a life of love, just as Christ loved us and
gave Himself up for us. Eph. 5:2

"You will call upon Me and come and pray to Me, and I will listen to you.
You will seek Me and find Me when you seek Me with all your heart."

Jer. 29:12-13

My soul finds rest in God alone;
My salvation comes from Him. Ps. 62:1

Delight yourself in the LORD, and He will give
you the desires of your heart. Ps. 37:4

The LORD is my light and my salvation–whom shall I fear?
The LORD is the stronghold of my life–of whom shall I be afraid?

Ps. 27:1

The LORD Himself goes before you and will be with you; He will never leave you nor forsake you.

Deut. 31:8

God is working in you, giving you the desire to
obey Him and the power to do what pleases Him.

Phil. 2:13

I can do everything through Christ,
who gives me strength.

Phil. 4:13

If you want to know what God wants you to do,
ask Him, and He will gladly tell you. James 1:5

Create in me a pure heart, O God, and renew
a steadfast spirit within me. Ps. 51:10

If anyone is in Christ, he is a new creation;
the old has gone, the new has come! 2 Cor. 5:17

Cast your cares on the LORD and He will sustain you.

Ps. 55:22

The LORD your God is with you, He is mighty
to save. He will take great delight in you,
He will quiet you with His love. Zeph. 3:17

The LORD is faithful to all His promises
and loving toward all He has made. Ps. 145:13

In You, O LORD, do I put my trust. Ps. 71:1

"Be strong and courageous. . . . The LORD your God
will be with you wherever you go." Josh. 1:9

Depend on the LORD in whatever you do,
and your plans will succeed. Prov. 16:3

Since we have been justified through faith, we have peace
with God through our LORD Jesus Christ.

Rom. 5:1

The LORD is my rock, my fortress and my deliverer;
my God is my rock, in whom I take refuge. Ps. 18:2

"If anyone would come after Me, he must deny himself
and take up his cross and follow Me." Matt. 16:24

The word of the LORD is right and true;
He is faithful in all He does. Ps. 33:4

The LORD is my strength, my shield from every
danger. I trust in Him with all my heart. Ps. 28:7

In Him we have redemption through His blood,
the forgiveness of sins, in accordance with
the riches of God's grace. Eph. 1:7

I trust in Your unfailing love. I will rejoice
because You have rescued me. Ps. 13:5

Live a life of love, just as Christ loved us and
gave Himself up for us. Eph. 5:2

"You will call upon Me and come and pray to Me, and I will listen to you. You will seek Me and find Me when you seek Me with all your heart."

Jer. 29:12-13

My soul finds rest in God alone;
My salvation comes from Him. Ps. 62:1